MODERN
FARM TRACTORS

Andrew Morland & Peter Henshaw

Motorbooks International
Publishers & Wholesalers

First published in 1997 by Motorbooks International Publishers & Wholesalers, 729 Prospect Avenue, PO Box 1, Osceola, WI 54020-0001 USA

Motorbooks International is a certified trademark, registered with the United States Patent Office

The information in this book is true and complete to the best of our knowledge. All recommendations are made without any guarantee on the part of the author or Publisher, who also disclaim any liability incurred in connection with the use of this data or specific details

We recognize that some words, model names and designations, for example, mentioned herein are the property of the trademark holder. We use them for identification purposes only. This is not an official publication

Motorbooks International books are also available at discounts in bulk quantity for industrial or sales-promotional use. For details write to Special Sales Manager at the Publisher's address

Library of Congress Cataloging-in-Publication Data Available

ISBN 0-7603-0155-7

On the front cover: The John Deere 8850 four-wheel-drive articulated tractor was the largest tractor ever produced by John Deere. It is easily distinguished from the less-powerful six-cylinder 8000 series four-wheel-drive tractors by its six headlights instead of four across the wider grill. It is powered by a John Deere intercooled and turbocharged 955-ci V-8 diesel engine that produces 300 PTO horsepower.

On the frontispiece: The Deutz D8006 was produced between 1971 and 1978 and sold well in North America. Deutz exported tractors from 1966 through main dealers in Atlanta, Georgia; Davenport, Iowa; and Columbus, Ohio.

On the title page: The AGCO-Allis 8630 is powered by a six-cylinder, air-cooled, 120 PTO horsepower engine. The tractor's synchromesh transmission has 24 forward and 12 reverse speeds.

On the back cover: The Ford FW-30 is powered by a Cummins 903-ci V-8 diesel engine that produces 205 drawbar horsepower. The fuel tank holds a useful 225 gallons.

Printed in Hong Kong

CONTENTS

ACKNOWLEDGMENTS

I thank the following companies and tractor dealers for their help in supplying technical information and historic photographs:

AGCO-Allis; John Deere; JCB; Massey Ferguson; New Holland; Renault; Valmet; G.A. Vowles (Landini dealer) in Somerset, England; Tincknells (John Deere dealer) in southwest England; J.M. Coles (SAME dealer) Avon, England; J.H. White (New Holland dealer) in west England; and Brookes and Vernons and Pharoah Communications.

I also thank the following people for their kind and enthusiastic help:

Mike Clarke, Edwin Badman, the Biss family, John Briscoe, Alan and Fiona Britten, Rod Laurie, Steve Mitchel, Alun Scott, Robert Salmon, Donald and Ruth Schaefer, Roger Thomas, Eric Tietz, Bruce Whittle, and Ray West.

Andrew Morland

The White 6215 is the most powerful of the 6000 series tractors. The 504.5-ci Cummins 215 PTO horsepower six-cylinder diesel engine is wastegated, turbocharged, and aftercooled.

ONE

AGCO

Allis-Chalmers

In the beginning, Allis-Chalmers didn't make tractors at all. In fact, if it hadn't been for the perseverance of General Otto Falk, it probably never would have gotten into tractors. The General took control of the troubled company in 1912, convinced that its future lay in the young and expanding tractor market. But its origins lay another half century back, when Milwaukee businessman Edward P. Allis bought the bankrupt Reliance Works for the princely sum of $22. It had been a thriving iron works, but collapsed in the Financial Panic of 1857. Over the next couple of decades, Allis proceeded to build it via takeovers, mergers (notably with Fraser & Chalmer), and plain shrewd practices. By 1905, iron, mining, steam, and electricity were all part of the Allis-Chalmers empire.

Unfortunately, such heavy industry was prone to alarming peaks and troughs, one of which plunged A-C back into bankruptcy in 1912. Receivers Delmar Call and General Falk were called in, and

they immediately set about rationalizing and streamlining. But to put A-C on a more stable footing, it needed access to a growing market. Falk owned a farm in Waukesha, Wisconsin, and he knew that the market for tractors was potentially huge.

With Falk's insight and determination, Allis-Chalmers began building tractors. Before long, the company prospered as a major farm tractor manufacturer. A-C's Model U, the first tractor to have pneumatic tires, and Model WC, which was built between 1933 and 1948, provided farmers with comfort and versatility. They were both highly successful. The WC's replacement, the WD, contained improvements like Two-Clutch Power Control, Traction Booster, and Powershift adjustable-track wheels.

These conveniences were needed, but the market also wanted something else—more power and a diesel option. As farms got bigger and incomes rose, farmers demanded bigger, more powerful tractors. A-C, to stay competitive in the industry, had no choice but to respond, and the WD got a more powerful gasoline

The AGCO-Allis 9690 is only available in all-wheel-drive form. Its power comes from the low-maintenance air-cooled Deutz turbocharged 584-ci diesel engine.

A 1995 AGCO-Allis 5670 with optional canopy pulls a Hesston 540 round baler. The 5670 uses the four-cylinder air-cooled 244-ci diesel and produces 63 PTO horsepower.

engine (Power Crater) plus a diesel option. Diesel was the other side of the power game; as well as more horsepower, buyers wanted the greater economy of diesel. Throughout the 1950s, the tractor makers responded with ever bigger engines, but in 1961, A-C came up with the ideal solution—the turbodiesel.

It was a milestone in tractor designing; bring the power of gasoline together with diesel economy.

Turbodiesels weren't unknown in 1961, but until then they had been restricted to aircraft and large trucks, so A-C's turbocharged tractor made quite a splash. It was named D19, and it had a 31 percent power boost over the naturally aspirated D17. With its bigger rear tires and long tall hood, the D19 looked the part of range leader, which was just what A-C needed.

This cross-section view of an Allis-Chalmers 8000 series tractor shows the front wheel assistance system which proved most popular. The two-wheel-drive model only accounted for 17 percent of the total production. Between 1981 and 1985, A-C sold 8,850 of the 8000 series.

But the market was changing fast, and only a couple of years after the D19 wowed the public, something even more powerful came. The D21 wasn't turbocharged, but used a massive 6.9 liter diesel to break the 100 hp barrier and take A-C into new territory. It used direct injection (the first Allis to do so) and was to be A-C's staple big diesel until the old A-C plant closed in 1985. The direct injection diesel had been a favorite in trucks for years, and it worked by injecting fuel straight into the combustion chamber, rather than into a pre-chamber. The result was noisier than indirect injection, but it was just as powerful and even more fuel-efficient. Matching the biggest-ever engine was a massive, square-rigged design that looked totally different to any previous A-C tractor. It was styled by the company's Industrial Design Department to look brutally big. So big was the D21 compared to older Allises that it also needed an all-new transmission and range of bigger implements to match.

Inevitably, it also acquired a turbocharger after another couple of years, which took power take-off (PTO) power up to 128 hp. It was one of the most powerful tractors you could buy. All this power made four-wheel-drive more attractive, and Allis-Chalmers experimented with hydrostatic front wheel assist on the later D21. This used a hydraulic pump and motor on the front axle to drive the front wheels when needed. However, it didn't work very well. If the driver fed too much power to the front wheels, they would spin; too little power, and they would have to be pushed along. All but one of the D21 hydrostatics was converted back to plain two-wheel-drive. The move to 4x4 was inevitable though, and mechanical front wheel assist was a popular option on later big A-Cs. As for the D21, it lasted until 1969, the last, and by far the biggest, of the D series.

The model One-Ninety was the next step in building large tractors. It incorporated many features of the D21, such as the low-pressure, high-volume hydraulics, large flat platform, and non-turbo direct injection diesels. These were part of a family of gas, liquid propane gas, and diesel engines based on the modular principle.

But even the One-Ninety couldn't meet the demands of the horsepower war. The most powerful One-Ninety diesel might boast 77.2 PTO hp, but it simply wasn't enough. The answer was simple: repeat the D19 experience and bolt on a turbocharger. The One-Ninety XT was the result, and it answered the critics in no uncertain terms, with over 93 hp at the PTO. This was big tractor power in a medium-sized package. The XT almost became a legend in its lifetime. Tractor pullers loved it, as the XT could be tweaked to produce 120 hp. And weighing less than 8,000 lb, it could just be stripped down to slip into the 7,000 lb class. It was a hit, and it proved that Allis-Chalmers had finally caught up with the horsepower race.

The One-Seventy and One-Eighty models came out in 1967. The first was really a straight replacement for the old D17, while the One-Eighty moved into the 60 hp class, another example of A-C offering extra power in a smaller tractor. Both carried over well-known Allis features from the D17—Traction

11

The articulated four-wheel-drive 4W-305 was the top of the A-C line between 1982 and 1985. It had a twin turbo 731-ci A-C six-cylinder diesel engine that was rated at 250 PTO horsepower.

Booster, Roll-Shift front axle, and others which had been around for years. One new thing was the Perkins 3.8-liter diesel for the One-Seventy. A-C's own D262 was out of production now, and equivalents from its new family of engines were deemed too expensive. In the now familiar pattern, the new tractors were soon given a power boost; after a couple of years, the one seventy-five and one eighty-five came in with 62 and 75 hp respectively. The one eighty-five was now almost as powerful as the One-Ninety, and outlived it. In fact, the one seventy-five and one eighty-five were to stay in production until 1981.

Tractor competition was fierce in the early 1970s, and A-C once again responded. When introduced in 1973, the "New Family" 7000 series certainly fulfilled expectations. It was powerful, up-to-date, and included a host of new features. Just as important, it had the capacity for further upgrades. To say that the 7000s were long-awaited would be an understatement. Design studies for a new series of 100-140 hp tractors had actually begun in the early 1960s, but they were held up when transmission maker Allison pulled out of the program in 1967, and it took another two years for things to get back up to speed.

Enginewise, the 7000s got a development of the now familiar A-C 3500, the 6.9-liter six-cylinder diesel that had first appeared in the D21. The 7030 produced 131 PTO hp, while the range-topping 7050 got an intercooled version of the same thing. With bypass oil filter and piston cooling, it gave 156 hp. With the demise of the Allison transmission, A-C had to come up with its own solution. It combined Power Director with a manual five-speed transmission, using 20 forward speeds, four in reverse, and a suitably impressive list of ratios for the spec sheet.

Another new feature was load-sensitive hydraulics. Standard practice had been to maintain full hydraulic pressure regardless of load, which of course wasn't always needed. The new A-C system allowed the pressure to vary according to load, and to "idle" when it wasn't needed; this saved power and fuel. The 7000 series batteries could be easily swung out for servicing; no more grubbing around in some inaccessible corner under the hood. The fueling point was easier to reach, too. The 7000s were also the first A-C tractors to be built under the company's Flexible Manufacturing system. But the most obvious new idea was the Acousta Cab. For several years, there had been a growing trend towards the use of cabs as a safety item, designed and built into the tractor, rather than bolted on as some dealer accessory after-thought. Safety was a serious subject, and it became an important factor in tractor sales.

That's why, when the 7000 appeared, it offered both ROPS (Roll Over Protective System) and the Acousta Cab. The latter was a response to concern about in-cab noise. Long-term exposure to engine roar and gear whine was proving to cause

A 1991 Deutz-Allis 9130 with power front axle assistance. the German-built Deutz air-cooled diesel engine has quick warm-up time and low maintenance costs.

occupational deafness in farmers. To make matters worse, some of the early cabs actually increased the noise level. But the Acousta Cab isolated the driver very effectively, and at 79.5 dB, it actually made the 7000s the quietest tractors in the business.

For once, Allis-Chalmers was able to forsee that one of its new tractors might need upgrading. Sure enough, only a year after the launch, both the 7030 and 7050 got 5 hp power boosts and were renamed 7040 and 7060 respectively. There was also a 7080 with the 6.9-liter engine that was given a higher rated speed (2,550rpm) and lots of internal changes. At the other end of the scale, a basic 7000 in the new style appeared in 1975. It really had more in common with the ageing 200 than the New Family, but used the Acousta Cab and new styling to good effect.

This 1996 AGCO-Allis 8630 has 120 PTO horsepower and two-wheel-drive. Here it pulls a Hesston 1160 mower/conditioner that can cut on the right and the left.

Meanwhile Allis-Chalmers hadn't neglected the mid-range tractors, knowing the One-Seventy/One-Eighty would sooner or later need replacing. The trouble was, it was becoming increasingly uneconomic to make cheaper tractors wholly in the US, and the only way around this was to import parts or complete tractors and stick the A-C badge on them. There was nothing new in this. The ED40 had been built in A-C's English factory, while the little One-Sixty (later the 6040) used many Renault parts. The 6000 series used the same principles, but this time the partner was Fiat. Fiat also supplied the smaller 5050 fully-built, while the A-C's 5040 came from UTB of Romania.

For the 6000s, Fiat supplied transmissions, front axles, and three-point hitches, all of which kept the price competitive. A-C still used its own 433T (3.3-liter) diesel, in either turbo or intercooled form, which produced the required 64 to 84 hp. Front-wheel assist, a sort of halfway effort to full four-wheel-drive, was a popular option, and more than one-third of the 6000s were ordered with it. The 6000 series was the last tractor ever to roll off the West Allis production line.

It was also the end for the 8000 series, which had replaced the 7000 in 1982. Basically an update on the same theme, the 8000 came in four

The electronic powershift transmission on the 1996 AGCO-Allis 9650 all-wheel-drive tractor provides 18 forward and 9 reverse speeds. The easy shuttle shifting from forward to reverse, without clutching, makes loading operations much easier.

This Deutz 6250V vineyard model wears European markings with no Allis identification. Power comes from the fuel efficient air-cooled four-cylinder Deutz diesel engine.

models: 8010 (107 hp, and the only one to use the 4.9-liter diesel), 8030 (134 hp, 6.9-liter), 8050 (152 hp, 6.9-liter intercooled), and the range-topping 8070 (171 hp, and a higher speed version of the 6.9). All of them benefited from an all-new cab, which was far bigger than the 7000's Acousta Cab. It had 24 percent more glass area (bigger than any rival), all-around visors, and a suspension seat which moved fore-aft as well as up-down. And of course, it was air conditioned. As on the smaller tractors, front-wheel assist was offered, though some buyers balked at the $7,500 option price. But the bigger the tractor, the more popular it was. Only 10 percent of 8070 customers opted for plain two-wheel-drive.

Unfortunately, the 8000 was introduced just as the worst post-war agricultural recession started to bite. It was no time to be selling expensive, high-tech tractors which few farmers could afford to buy. So no one was too surprised when A-C sold its tractor business to Deutz of Germany. Deutz had no wish to

build tractors in the US, and closed the West Allis plant shortly before Christmas in 1985.

But it wasn't the end of the Allis name. The new Deutz-Allis concern did restart tractor production in 1989 (though these had nothing in common with the A-C tractors), and the following year was itself taken over by the giant AGCO, which had started life as a management buy-out of the Gleaner concern. The result, by the mid-1990s, was a full line-up of tractors with clear Deutz influence, still carrying the Allis name.

Smallest of the new tractors is the 5650/5660, both powered by a 3.0-liter three-cylinder air-cooled diesel. Deutz, renowned for its air-cooled engines, has evidently left its mark. There are 45 and 55 hp

NEXT: The AGCO-Allis 9655 all-wheel-drive tractor shows its excellent turning circle. It is powered by the Series 40 liquid-cooled 466-ci six-cylinder turbocharged engine. Horsepower at the PTO is 155.

This Deutz-Allis 6250V vineyard model was built for the North American market. Note the addition of the Allis name on the radiator shell.

versions, both of which have the same 12-speed transmission, creeper range (for ultra low speed work) and four-wheel-drive option. Next up is the 5600 with a four-cylinder 4.0-liter diesel. Again air-cooled, with direct injection, this one produces either 63 or 72 hp (in the top models, 45 and 55 hp options were also available) and has cast-iron heads and crankcase. Like its little brother, the basic transmission is a 12-speed (four-speed gearbox with three ranges) though there are options for 16 or even 24 forward ratios. The 6600 series was really a row crop version of the 5600, and at launch the two tractors shared 72 percent of their components. Again, you could have two- or four-wheel-drive, and once again

a four-cylinder air-cooled diesel provided the power, up to 81 hp in the 6690. It was a Deutz engine of course, part of the German firm's legacy to Allis.

By the time you got to the 7600 series, you were into serious power. The basic 7600 used a five-cylinder Deutz engine of 89 hp; the 7630 had a 115 hp six, while the 7650 was turbocharged to give 128 hp. Standard transmission was a 24-speed forward, 12-speed reverse setup, but a 30-speed system was optional on the 7650. There were all the usual features found on upper mid-range tractors: hydrostatic steering, 540/1,000rpm power take-offs, and an air conditioned cab. The 8600 was no higher up in the power stakes (103 or 120 hp) but had an altogether

A Deutz D8006 built in the mid-1970s is still at work in Wisconsin. The Deutz air-cooled engine, with no water to freeze up in the coldest winter, was popular with dairy farmers in northern climates.

higher-tech approach. There was an electronic speed control; in theory, you set the desired speed, and the tractor would maintain it regardless of load. The driver was faced by an impressive array of instruments, including tachometer (electronic, inevitably), fuel, engine temperature, oil pressure, and battery condition, while a schematic diagram of the 8600 replaced the usual confusing bank of warning lights.

But it was in the 9000 series that electronics really took over. This was the future of high-tech tractor design, as electronic control of the three-point hitch and other functions could sense when things were going wrong and correct them, taking the onus off the driver. AGCO-Allis' version was the Electronic Control System that monitored the rear differential lock, four-wheel-drive, PTO, transmission, and hydraulic pressure. If necessary, it would switch on the differential lock or reduce hydraulic pressure if damage was threatened. You might have thought all this reduced the driver to the role of machine minder, who had to steer occasionally. But as any worker in a paperless electronic office will tell you, the reverse is true. Take the electronic three-point hitch. In the old days, it was possible to control the depth and draft of the implement, its rate of drop, and linkage height. Then came the information revolution. All these electronics brought digital read-outs of engine, ground, PTO speed, the amount of acres covered, and tire slippage. So in some ways life had got more complicated. The engine options certainly were, with liquid-cooled alternatives to the Deutz sixes. These were big engines too (the biggest available at launch)—7.6- or 8.7-liter liquid-cooled (all turbocharged) up to a 9.6-liter air-cooled with just under 200 hp. Once again, Allis-badged tractors were up to the minute. Few would have predicted that when the factory closed down in 1985.

The Perkins 6-liter engine in the Landini Legend 130 is rated at 123 horsepower. The British Perkins engines have been manufactured at the Landini factory in Italy since 1956 under a licensing agreement.

The 1987 Deutz-Allis 6260 uses a four-cylinder air-cooled Deutz diesel engine. This North American market tractor has Deutz-Allis written on the cab. In the European market, the name Deutz-Fahr is written on the cab.

Deutz

Few European tractor makers have achieved worldwide fame, but Deutz is one of them. It was an old firm, established in 19th century Germany, which produced its first diesel engine in 1898, only a few years after Rudolph Diesel completed his first prototype. Its first tractor (the Deutz Motor Plough) appeared in 1907, and it brought the diesel engine and tractor together in 1924. Since then, Deutz had made something of a specialty of air-cooled diesels, unique in the tractor business.

Deutz entered the US market in 1966, not just with tractors, but with a whole engine range. In general, these odd new tractors were well received. Among the choices in 1971 were the D5506 (with a four-cylinder 3.3-liter diesel with 49 hp) and the D8006 (5.6-liter, six-cylinder, 73 hp). Apart from the air cooling, they were relatively conventional, with 8- or 16-speed transmissions. However, they were definitely noisier than the opposition. According to figures from the renowned Nebraska tests, the D8006 generated 98.0 dB(A) against 88.5 for the equivalent I-H.

After the take-over of Allis-Chalmers, Deutz's own range was renamed Deutz-Allis. Typical were the 6200 series, offered in vineyard, orchard, or low-profile forms as well as the standard ones. There was two- or four-wheel-drive, and the air-cooled diesel was available in two forms: 65 hp 3.8-liter or 71 hp 4.1 liter. Like many low and mid-range tractors of the time, the steering was hydrostatic, while the transmission was a simple four-speed gearbox with three ranges. Air conditioning was standard in the flat floor Star Cab, and if you didn't opt for that, rollover protection system was standard.

But the 1990s could well spell the end for air-cooled tractor engines. Just as emissions legislation had been applied to cars, it is now being extended to off-road machinery. Deutz forsaw this and realized that its own air-cooled diesels would have great difficulty meeting both noise and emissions standards on

The interior of the Landini Legend 130 engine compartment. The air filter and battery are in front of the oil cooler and water radiator.

the horizon. For the first time, there would have to be a water-cooled Deutz tractor.

When it came, the Agratron was about as up-to-the-minute as it could be, with that low-nose look that has become synonymous with the latest tractors. More to the point, Deutz was able to claim 90 percent all-around visibility for the new cab, with glass reaching right down to the floor on three sides. Even the sunroof was glass, for easier observation similar to a front end loader. There was air conditioning, (now CFC

The four-cylinder 3870-cc Perkins diesel engine in the Landini 9880 is rated at 88 PTO horsepower at 540rpm.

free), and all the controls were bright, simple, and color-coded.

But the real news was the engines—a new range of four- and six-cylinder turbocharged diesels whose main innovation was a separate high-pressure injection pump for each cylinder, operated directly by the camshaft. Another interesting point was that the entire range was biodiesel compatible. This rapeseed oil-based fuel has found favor in many parts of Europe, being renewable and far less polluting than conventional diesel. The engine range started with a 3.2-liter 68 hp unit and went up to the intercooled 7.1-liter six with 145 hp.

The Agrotron wasn't a complete range, but only a few months after its launch, Deutz was promising that it would be extended both up and down. The company might have had to abandon its enthusiasm for air-cooled tractors, but it seems determined enough to make the best of a new era.

Landini

Landini's origins, like those of so many other tractor makers, lay in the 19th century agricultural machinery business. Giovanni Landini was a blacksmith's apprentice who went into business on his own account in 1884, though he didn't start developing a tractor until the early 1920s. Landini never saw the tractor project come to fruition—he died in 1924—but his sons carried on the business. They announced a 30 hp semi-diesel tractor the following year.

Landini the company was very attached to semi-diesels, clinging to the concept long after most rivals had abandoned it. Basically, semi-diesels were simpler and cheaper to make than a true diesel, relying on a hot bulb rather than solely on compression ignition to ignite the fuel. They were also smokey, rough, and woefully inefficient. As an example, the Super Landini of 1934 needed a massive single cylinder of over 14 liters to produce its 40 hp.

But by the mid 1950s, Landini was close to collapse. Too much reliance on the semi-diesel, when rivals had forged ahead with true diesels and Ferguson-influenced designs, meant Landini tractors were looking old and outmoded. The company probably owes its survival to Dr. Flavio Fadda, who, soon after he took control, negotiated a licensing deal with Perkins. Landini would make two-, three-, and four-cylinder Perkins diesels under license to power a new generation of modern tractors. The new range of R4500, L7000, and F300 were all successful, and within a few years, the old semi-diesels were no more. Another innovation at the time was the crawler C4000, announced in 1957. Designed with the hillier parts of the home market in mind, the C crawler did well too, after a protracted development. Since then, Landini has remained prominent in the crawler market, and all its tractors are Perkins powered.

Successful as the new tractors were, they couldn't hide the fact that Landini was still a small

The Massey Ferguson 374S is a narrow, adjustable-track fruit tractor and is ideal for vineyards and fruit crop cultivation. It is powered by a Perkins four-cylinder 3860-cc diesel engine that is rated at 62 horsepower.

The Massey Ferguson 6180 is powered by a Perkins 6-liter turbocharged six-cylinder diesel engine. The Dynashift transmission has 32 forward and 32 reverse speeds, with synchro shuttle and powershift.

company in a market full of big rivals. So the takeover by Massey-Ferguson in 1960 was hardly unwelcome. It gave M-F access to the Italian market and crawler range and Landini financial security. Landini was able to set up a new plant in Aprilia to make industrial size crawlers and in 1973 launched the 6/7/8500 tractor range with a 12+4 transmission. Four years later, it came up with Europe's first 100 hp tractor with a conventional layout and four-wheel-drive.

The Massey Ferguson 362 four-wheel-drive tractor uses a Perkins four-cylinder engine that produces 62 horsepower from 3860cc. This lightweight tractor has a high PTO power-to-weight ratio, which is ideal where reduced soil compaction and minimal damage to ground or grassland is paramount.

This cross-section of a Massey Ferguson 6100 series tractor shows the 32-speed Dynashift transmission and four-wheel-drive system. The 6100 series uses the four-cylinder and six-cylinder Perkins diesel engines. It is also available, with the same mechanical specifications, in a "high visibility model," which features a streamlined sloping hood that is ideal for operating front-mounted equipment.

Through the 1980s, there were more diversions. Landini got into orchard tractors in 1982 (Landini recently claimed a one-third share of this world-wide market) and created a vineyard range in 1986. Like the crawlers, the vineyard tractors are also sold with a Massey-Ferguson badge in some marekts. The mid-range tractors were replaced in 1988 by the 60-70-80 series, which boasted a 24+12 transmission.

One current equivalent to those mid-rangers is the Blizzard 85, which was part of a major range renewal in 1992. It uses the Perkins 4.248 in non-turbo form, a simple 4.0-liter four-cylinder direct injection engine with 80 hp at 2,200rpm (at the flywheel) and 208 lb ft at 1,400rpm. The basic transmission has 12 forward and 12 reverse speeds with syncromesh reverse shuttle, but there are creeper underdrive and overdrive (25 mph) options to double the number of forward speeds. Four-wheel-drive is another option, as are the inevitable electronic aids

(Landtronic ELC in this case), though digital instrumentation is standard. Further up the range is the 9880 with a smaller, but turbocharged, Perkins of 3.9-liters. The transmission is basically the same as the one in the 85, again with four-wheel-drive, creeper, and underdrive and overdrive options.

The Landini Legend tractor is in a different class, the six-cylinder 100 hp-plus class. All three models use Perkins' 6.0-liter 1006 diesel in 110, 123, or 138 hp form. In fact, these relatively small power differences are all that really set these tractors apart. They all have a transmission with a bewildering variety of ratios. Four-wheel-drive is standard, as it is on just about every tractor of this power, as is air conditioning on the two top models. It's all a long way from the Landini brothers' first semi-diesel.

The massive Massey Ferguson 9240 uses the Cummins 6CTA8.3 six-cylinder turbocharged and aftercooled 504-ci diesel engine. The engine is rated at 240 brake horsepower at 2,200rpm; maximum PTO horsepower is 210. The electronically controlled powershift transmission has 18 forward and 9 reverse gears.

A Massey Ferguson 3655 tractor pulls a New Holland 640 Bale Command round baler. The owner and contractor is Colin Targett of Somerset, Great Britain.

Behind the tractors, Landini was subject to all the usual corporate maneuverings. In 1989, M-F sold 66 percent of its Landini shares to a holding company, which in turn was taken over by another holding group. In 1993, that group had a financial crisis, forcing Landini back to partners closer to its own roots. The M-F link is still there, but ARGO took over in 1994, and there have been agreements with Iseki and AGCO to develop and sell the tractor range. The bottom line for Landini is that its expertise in crawlers and respected name in the Italian market should ensure that it survives into the next century, whoever owns it.

Massey-Ferguson

Massey-Ferguson has grown as much out of corporate shenanigans as producing tractors. Mergers, splits, agreements, and arguments have littered its history, shaped by strong individuals like Henry Ford, Harry Ferguson, and Frank Perkins. But despite the checkered past, it survived, and in the mid-1980s could claim to be the largest tractor manufacturer in the western world, with factories in France and Canada as well as Britain. When it was taken over by the AGCO Corporation in 1994, it more than doubled its new owner's turnover.

Here is a quick history of Massey-Ferguson. In 1847, Daniel Massey sets up business; Alanson

The Massey Ferguson 2685 was built at Beauvais in France. Here Harvey Maunder collects grain from a Massey Ferguson 31XP combine.

Harris establishes his business ten years later. As established makers of Canadian agricultural machinery, they merge in 1891. Massey-Harris makes its first tractor in 1919. Harry Ferguson perfects his three-point linkage in the 1930s, and David Brown starts making the Ferguson tractor for him in 1936. Distrust grows between Brown and Ferguson, and the agreement ends in 1938, just as Ferguson's new deal with Ford comes to fruition. Based on a handshake, Ford builds the 9N, based around the Ferguson system. In 1946, Harry seals another deal, with the Standard company, to produce the Ferguson TE tractor in Banner Lane, Coventry. Meanwhile, Ford announces its 8N, breaking Ferguson patents; a four-year legal battle ensues, and Ferguson sets up his own factory in Detroit. In 1953, Harry Ferguson sells his tractor interests to Massey-

Harris, and Massey-Ferguson is born, with Harry as chairman and engineering advisor. He resigns soon afterwards (a disagreement over his planned TE60) and concentrates on research into four-wheel-drive for cars. Meanwhile, Massey-Ferguson gets on with the business of merging the "red" and "gray" sides of the business and buys up Perkins in 1959 and Landini the year after. The company changes its corporate name to Varity in 1986 and sells M-F tractor business to AGCO in 1994.

Having gotten the politics out of the way, we can look at the tractors. It's arguable that the modern era for Massey-Ferguson began in 1962 with the DX program, which as far as the farming public was concerned emerged at the 1964 Smithfield show as the "Red Giants," the MF 135, 165, and 175. According to Michael Williams, the new tractors were a major

A White 6105 uses a White 686SL loader to stack round bales. Power comes from the six-cylinder naturally aspirated 366-ci diesel engine.

project involving a million hours of designing and testing, with all-new or substantially redesigned machines coming out the other end. The hydraulics were unchanged, though the control was repositioned on the right-hand side of the gearbox. There was also a new feature, Pressure Control, which allowed for weight transfer from implements, and auxiliary hydraulics for operating hydraulic equipment off the tractor. This was an option at first, but was soon made standard on the 165 and 175.

Engine options were little changed. The baby 135 used the same three-cylinder Perkins as the old 35X, producing the same 45.5 bhp. Likewise, the 165's 3.3-liter 58 bhp four was carried over. Both the 135 and 150 had gasoline options, but even among smaller tractors, diesel was becoming the major choice now. The 175 used a bigger 3.8-liter Perkins

of 66 bhp. What all the Red Giants shared was new squared-off styling which Allis-Chalmers had already used to good effect. It worked for M-F as well, as the new line was very successful. There were various detail improvements over the years, including engine upgrades in 1968 (the 175 got a 4.0-liter engine with 72.5 bhp), safety cabs in 1970, and oil-cooled brakes the year after. In 1972, M-F introduced a longer wheelbase version, with a 6-inch spacer between the transmission and center housings. Named the 148, 168, and 188 (equivalent to the 135, 165, and 185), these gave a more spacious driving position and greater stabilty.

By the early 1970s, M-F could no longer ignore the market for massive four-wheel-drive tractors with four equal-sized wheels. Although designed for the sweeping acreages of American and Canadian

The White 6195 is powered by the Cummins turbocharged and aftercooled 504.5-ci engine rated at 200 PTO horsepower at 2,200rpm.

farms, these were starting to find favor in Europe as well. Massey's response was the 1200. Canadian-built, it naturally used the Ferguson System and three-point linkage, and was the first M-F with four-wheel-drive since the war. It was soon followed by the 1500, whose 9.4-liter Caterpillar V-8 diesel produced 153 hp at 3,000rpm, and the 1800 (8.3-liter V-8, 179 hp). These were uprated after a short time into the 1505 and 1805, which were in production from 1975 until being replaced by the 4000 series. But the most successful of these 4x4 tractors was the original 1200 and uprated 1250, with 105 and 112 hp, respectively.

Meanwhile, the Red Giants were nearing the end, and in 1975 were replaced by the 200 series; the 135 gave way to the 235, and so on. They used the same front-end styling as the new 500 series, but the 235 stuck with the Perkins three-cylinder diesel for the first year. It was soon uprated into a 240 (45 hp) and the range then progressed in familiar steps via the 255 (3.3 liter, 51 hp), 265 (3.9-liter 61 hp), 275 (4.0-liter 67 hp), and 285 (5.2-liter 82 hp). The latter later became a 290, while an 88 hp 298 appeared in early 1981.

But although the 200 series went up to relatively high outputs, they were relatively low specification, affordable tractors. The 500 series, unveiled to the public at the Royal Show in England the year after the 200, covered much the same power range, but was a very different tractor. It showed just how varied and niche-ridden the tractor market had become, that there was room for two ranges of the same power to run alongside each other. The difference was that the 500 was genuinely new where the 200 was an update of an older, simpler tractor. For starters, it had an all-new cab designed to reduce noise to a minimum. The whole structure

Working hard are a White 6085 tractor with AGCO 640 loader and a White 6125 tractor with New Idea spreader. The 6085 uses a four-cylinder 244-ci 80.2 PTO horsepower engine. The 6125 uses a six-cylinder 359-ci 124 PTO horsepower engine. Both engines are turbocharged.

was isolated from the chassis by anti-vibration mountings, while all controls (apart from the gear levers) used remote linkages (rather than being directly linked to the rest of the machine) to further dampen noise and vibration. It was roomy, with a big glass area and plenty of heating/ventilation capacity. New instruments and new front-end styling with recessed headlamps emphasized that this was a new tractor.

The hydraulics came in for improvement too, with an optional auxiliary system able to deliver 7.9 gpm through spool valves on single or double acting operation. If you combined the High Flow, linkage and auxiliary pumps, up to 13.75 gpm was available

for external machinery. The Ferguson System itself was upgraded, the linkage pump having larger control valves and galleries while the Pressure Control and response systems were combined; the result was greater capacity and easier servicing. Two-speed power take-offs were becoming common in mid-range tractors, so of course the 500 had to have it. A direct drive shaft gave 1,000rpm; a six-spline one gave 540rpm, via a reduction gear set. Different splines made it impossible to put the wrong shaft in and damage valuable machinery by driving it at the wrong speed.

There was hydrostatic power steering (which meant no mechanical linkage between cab and wheels), and transmission options were an eight-speed or M-F's Multi-Power 12-speed. A five-model range (from the 47 hp 550 to 88 hp 595) lasted until 1981, when it was replaced by the 600 series.

Although the 500 had been built at the Banner Lane works, its successor was a joint project between Coventry and the M-F plant at Beauvais in France. It really represented a move upmarket from the 500, dropping the 47 and 60 hp entry-level models and later adding a six-cylinder option at the top of the range. There were three versions at first: the 66 hp 675, 77 hp 690, and 88 hp 698, though the latter was to receive a different turbocharged engine in 1984, with 90 hp. The six-cylinder 699 gave 95 hp. Only five years after the 500's debut, its wonder cab needed another update. On the 600, air conditioning joined the options list; M-F claimed better ventilation and less noise, while the doors were forward-hinged. The leveling lever and auto hitch control joined the others inside the cab and the roof could open for extra ventilation. There was also the option of four-wheel-drive across the whole range and better engine access, thanks to hinged panels.

Some of these features also trickled down to the 200 series, which was updated at the same time. In fact, this once simple tractor found itself being upgraded in several ways—by 1986, only the entry-level 230 was cabless and four-wheel drive was availalbe on all except that one and the 240. The mid-range 250 (47 hp) was said to the be the first of that power with power steering and oil-cooled brakes, while the 12-speed Multi-Power transmission was standard on the top-range 200s.

While all this was going on, Beauvais was busy with an all-new range of Topline tractors. Commonly known as the 2640, 2680, and 2720, these were all-new and were one step up from the 600. The gearbox had 16 forward and 12 reverse speeds and incorporated a speed shift which allowed a range change under load without using the clutch. Like the optional four-wheel-drive, this was push-button operated. There were inboard disc brakes, a hydraulically oper-

ated differential lock, and a rubber-mounted cab. The diesels were all Perkins (having one's own engine supplier tended to make this decision an easy one) ranging from a basic 110 hp, via a 130 hp turbo to 147 hp with intercooling. Launched in 1979, the 2000 series was updated with electronic linkage control as the 2005 in 1985.

Its ultimate replacement, the 3000, appeared the following year. It was basically a range of lower-powered tractors but with up-to-the-minute transmission and linkage control. Every model, from the 71 hp 3050 to the 107 hp 3090, had the electronic linkage control. This was no more than most manufacturers were offering, though Autotronic versions gave some automatic operation of the differential lock, four-wheel-drive, and PTO engagement. If you opted for the Datatronic version, there was a digital display of vital functions in the cab, and also a wheel-slip control; the driver could limit the degree of slip to maximize traction. The speed shift which first appeared on the 2000 was optional, but there was a new PTO with five alternative drives.

In 1987, M-F did the obvious and brought in higher-powered versions of the 3000 to replace the 2000. Power choices were uprated slightly to 113 hp, 133 hp (turbo), and 150 bhp (intercooler). There were more substantial increases in 1990, when all three were replaced by the 3645 (142 hp) and 3655 (155 hp). There was even, horror of horrors, a non-Perkins engine option, the 180 hp Valmet. But there were new features from Perkins too. All but the highest-powered 3000s used Perkins' new 1000 series six-cylinder direct-injection diesel. It centered around something called the Quadram system, basically a combustion bowl in the piston crown with four lobes to optimise mixing. According to Perkins, this quickened combustion and evened out combustion pressure peaks. The result, it said, was more torque at low speeds. The last major change to the 3600 came in 1992 with the Dynashift transmission, which used a four-speed epicyclic gear system mounted

The White 6124 Quadrashift tractor has a transmission with 32 forward and reverse speeds. The tractor can go from a crawl to 22.5 mph on the highway. It is powered by the 359-ci six-cylinder 124 PTO horsepower Cummins diesel engine.

ahead of the basic 8-speed gearbox. The result was 32 speeds (forward or reverse), 24 of which were clutchless changes.

While these big Beauvais-built tractors advanced, the smaller ones from Banner Lane were developing too. The 600 series was replaced by the 300 in 1986, one new feature being the availability of the Perkins 1000 (Quadram and all) on the 104 hp 399. The most complex transmission was still a 12-speed, but it was now an all-syncromesh shuttle gearbox, with all functions for forward and reverse controlled by one lever. Since then, an 18-ratio speed shift has become available, offering road speeds up to 25 mph. The range is still a big one from the 62 bhp 365 (still with the familiar Perkins 4.236 in non-turbo form) to the 104 hp 399, while the little 135's role is kept up by the three-cylinder 342 and 352. There's still a choice of Low Profile or HiLine cabs (the latter with extra soundproofing and an air conditioning option), and a more recent addition is the Forestry model. It's based on the standard 390, but with things like standard four-wheel-drive and reversible seat.

Most recently, all 3000/3600s have been dropped in favor of the new 6100/8100 with a massive range from 80 to 200 hp. Most of them feature the latest generation of M-F's electronic controls. Datatronic II, for example, now offers up to 22 functions, including four memories, a print-out facility, and even cost-analysis. But these are no longer the top of the M-F range. The new 9240 (which went on sale in early 1995) is bigger still, with a turbocharged/intercooled Cummins diesel of 8.2-liters and 240 bhp. It weighs nearly ten tons and has four-wheel-drive and a passenger seat.

The White 6215 uses the powerful Cummins six-cylinder 504.5-ci turbocharged and aftercooled 215 PTO horsepower engine.

White

White's corporate history is almost as checkered as Massey-Ferguson, and certainly as complex. The origins weren't in White at all, but Oliver. Scotsman James Oliver set up a farm equipment business in 1855, and son Joseph oversaw the merger with three other firms (including tractor pioneers Hart-Parr) in 1929. Oliver tractors, like the lightweight Row-Crop or GM two-stroke-powered Super 99 diesel, won many adherents.

But in 1960, the Iowa-based firm was taken over by White, which was renowned as makers of big-rig trucks but with no experience in tractors. White seemed determined to get into the agricultural business, buying up Cockshutt and Minneapolis-Moline, as well as Oliver. For the first few years, these respected names and their color schemes remained in place, but the White name gradually took over.

And it stuck, despite the parent company's decision to sell its farm equipment business in 1980. The new owners (Texas Investment Corp.) kept it only five years before selling out to the Allied Products Corporation. It was merged with New Idea in 1987 and in 1991 was taken over by the burgeoning AGCO empire, which in a few short years has risen from a management buy-out to become one of the biggest tractor makers in the world.

If you could pinpoint a time when the White name subsumed all the others, it would be 1974. The new range of Field Boss tractors came with the White name and its corporate gray and silver color scheme. Many machines went under this name in the 1970s, ranging from the 2-30 and 2-35 (actually made by Iseki of Japan, but sold through White dealers) to the 4-180, with its 10.4-liter Caterpillar V-8 diesel of 180 hp (and replaced by the 210 hp 4-210 in 1982). Many of the smaller ones were built by Iseki, up to a 75 hp tractor that was sold up to 1988. But White's own tended to be big six-cylinder machines like the 2-110 and 4-175.

A new range of tractors in 1987 saw the end of the Field Boss name (no great loss) and the arrival of the 100, 120, 140, and 160. Power spread from 92 hp to 160, and all of these used a Cummins six-cylinder diesel. The transmission was an 18 forward/6 reverse unit; four-wheel-drive with manual front differential lock was optional. The following year the renewal process spread downwards with the 60, 80, and 100. The 80's 3.9-liter Cummins qualified it as the first sub-90 hp tractor to be built in America for a decade. In a fit of patriotism, White named this range the New American Series.

Today, White's range centers around the 6000 series, which has done well from its access to the big range of ACGO dealers. The four-cylinder 6065 and 6085 have kept White's presence in the lower-medium market, but you get the feeling that, with that name on the hood, the 6100 series sixes have more in common with White's legacy.

In the mid-1990s, these started with the 6125—124 hp from the 5.9-liter Cummins at a 2,200rpm rated speed. An intercooled 142 hp version of the same engine powers the 6145, while the other 6000s use an 8.3-liter Cummins, from 175 hp to 215, depending on whether it's intercooled. The transmission controls were electronic and, as is commonplace on big modern tractors, electronics also oversaw the shifting, to ensure no damage could be done to this expensive piece of machinery. The standard range was 18 forward speeds and 9 in reverse, but adding the optional creeper range brought that to 36 and 18. The more sophisticated Quadrashift came later, but the 18-speed was still available, and from 1995 gained electronic control for the three-point hitch. Oliver might be no more, but its new parent lived on.

TWO

CASE INTERNATIONAL

Case International is one of the true pioneers. Like Allis-Chalmers, its main constituent parts—J.I. Case and International Harvester—were in business well before the turn of the century. And again like Allis-Chalmers, it has expanded by acquisition. Buying the American Tractor Company in 1957 took it into the world of crawlers. Among conventional tractor makers, David Brown, as well as International, came under the Case wing, while in 1986 the company bought out Steiger. J.I. Case made his name with a grain thresher in 1842 and followed it up with a portable steam engine in 1869. His company even attempted to get an early toehold in the new tractor market with the Paterson, but that failed before going on sale. It took Case another twenty years to have another go at gasoline tractors. At about the same time, International Harvester (itself formed by a merger) launched its Titan and Mogul tractor lines. Neither company was an outstanding innovator, but both were successful, respected tractor makers.

Now of course, everything is sold as a Case International. Until fairly recently, the lower and mid-range was covered by the 85 series. Like many rivals, it offered two alternative cabs, a lower spec Low Profile L to fit into lower barns and an XL Control Center with heater and rubber mounting, though you still had to pay extra for air conditioning. The aptly named L Economy Cab didn't even have a heater at all! Whichever model you went for, standard transmission was a simple 8-speed syncromesh, though it was possible to upgrade to a 16x8 powershift. The doubling of ratios came from the powershift (now virtually an industry standard), allowing a 17 percent ratio change in any gear at full power. A forward/reverse shuttle change and mechanical four-wheel-drive were also optional on the bigger tractors. In every case [sic] the engine was the company's own, ranging from the three-cylinder 45 hp (flywheel) 385 to the 82 hp 885.

The current equivalent Case I-H is the 3200/4200 series, really a modernized version of the

A 1996 Case International 5140 Maximum Plus. All 5000 series tractors have four-wheel-drive, power shuttle synchromesh transmission, and Case's own unique Max-O-Draulic hydraulics.

The engine in this 1970 Case Agri King 1070 is a six-cylinder 451-ci diesel unit that produces 108 horsepower at 2,100rpm.

same thing. In fact, it's an interesting example of how tractors are updated—more power, more cab features, but no radical changes. To take the engines first, the 45 hp three has been dropped, and the solitary 3220 uses the bigger 2.9-liter three-cylinder with 52 hp at a rated speed of 2,180rpm. At the other end of the scale, the 4.4-liter four has been tur-

bocharged to give 92 hp. Surprisingly, the basic transmission is still the 8x4 system, with the same shuttle and powershift options as before. The cab, though, is very different—more space, better visibility, and digital instrumentation are the most obvious changes. Less obvious is the optional air suspension seat (increasingly adopted as the best means of giving

This International Farmall 1256, built between 1967 and 1969, is still at work 30 years later in southern Wisconsin. The 406.9-ci six-cylinder turbocharged International-Harvester diesel engine is rated at 116 PTO horsepower.

a decent ride), while there's still the choice of XL and Low Profile (no Economy these days) cabs.

The 5100 covers the next class up, starting with the 92 hp turbo four. The rest of the range uses a 5.9-liter six-cylinder engine in either aspirated (100 hp at the flywheel) or turbo (110/125 hp) form. Naturally enough, the transmission is more sophisticated than

the 4200's. A shuttle is standard across the range while a three-speed powershift is standard on the higher-powered tractors. There's also a creeper range option which gives 24 forward and 20 reverse speeds, enabling the tractor to inch along at just 400 yards per hour. The standard transmission gives a 19 mph top speed, but like many rivals, this Case has a 25

A Case International 1494 pulls a load of bales back to the barn. This 1988 model is powered by a four-cylinder diesel engine rated at 78 PTO horsepower.

mph option to reduce time spent on the road. Like so many modern tractors, the 5100 has a sloping hood for better visibility.

At the top of the conventional Case I-H range comes the 7200 Magnum. Just a taste of the figures is enough to show that tractors are still getting bigger and more powerful by the year. Five models, all using an 8.3-liter turbo six, range from 155 hp to an inter-cooled 264 hp. All have four-wheel-drive, powershift, shuttle, and a 24x6 transmission. An electronic hitch control is featured too, but it's no more than buyers expect in this class. But even the Magnum isn't the biggest Case I-H you can buy. The less evocatively named 4894 is the company's current super-tractor, the sort that sell in tiny numbers in Europe, but

makes more sense in the vast fields of North America. International actually had an entrant in this class over 20 years ago, but did it the easy way by getting super-tractor specialists Steiger to build it for them. One interesting point is that the current super-tractors aren't vastly more powerful than the originals, and in fact the 4894 has the same 300 hp as its 1975 equiv-alent, along with 845 lb ft of torque. The transmis-sion too is limited to a three-speed powershift plane-tary system with four speed ranges in each, reflecting the different transmission needs of the super-tractors. But one thing that sets it apart from conventional tractors is the steering. You can steer the front pair of wheels from the steering wheel or the rear pair by a rocker switch. Or switch to four-wheel steer mode

This Case International 5150, shown here at the European Plowing Championships, shows off the power of the latest high-torque 5.9-liter six-cylinder turbocharged Case engine.

and the steering wheel controls all four wheels on the ground. Best of all, a crab selection allows the tractor to move diagonally in a straight line.

Steiger

In 1957, Douglas and Maurice Steiger did something that would be almost impossible today—they entered the tractor business. Forget about corporate take-over or massive capital backing; the Steiger brothers needed a large, powerful four-wheel-drive tractor to use on their Minnesota farm. No manufacturer was offering one, so they made one themselves. In fairy tale fashion, neighbors liked the look of it, and asked for copies. Business blossomed.

It was partly a case of coming along at the right time. There was a big demand for bigger tractors, yet none of the established makers were offering enough power or four-wheel-drive. There was the Harris 4x4, but that wasn't really powerful enough, and many US farmers resorted to crawler tractors, which had the power but were very expensive. In England, one farmer got round the problem by mating two Fordson Majors together; the twin-engined Doe Triple D went on sale in 1957. Steigers' solution was different; it had four massive wheels, with a big diesel overhanging the front pair. The machine was articulated in the middle to give a good turning circle, and it could cope with massive acreages faster than any conventional tractor. The super-tractor was born.

The power shifting transmission on the Case International 4210 gives 16 forward and 8 reverse speeds.

The Steiger Panther ST310 is powered by a Cummins NH-855T. This turbocharged diesel six-cylinder 855-ci engine is rated at 310 horsepower with 261 drawbar horsepower.

That first one used a 238 hp Detroit diesel six of 6.9 liters, but as Steiger sales grew (120 annually within a few years of starting), so did their tractors. The top of the 1960s range was the 3300, with a 9.3-liter Detroit diesel V-8, 16 forward speeds, and an all-up weight of 31,000 lb. There were small V-6 and four-cylinder versions as well.

Of course, it wasn't long before the big manufacturers got in on the act, and there were other four-wheel-drive specialists like Knudson, MRS, and Woods & Copeland. In any case, one quick way for the majors to enter this market was to ask the specialists for help. In 1973, Steiger found itself assembling International Harvester's 4366 (I-H had bought into Steiger the previous year), which was followed up by the 4368, complete with I-H's own 13.0-liter V-8 diesel. And as the original super-tractor, the Steiger kept on developing. In 1974, for example, it was offering Caterpillar engines in its Bearcat II and Cougar II tractors—a 10.4-liter V-8 and six-cylinder turbo, respectively. Biggest of the lot was the Tiger II— 14.7 liter, 270 hp turbocharged Cummins V-8. Sadly for Steiger's independence, it could not survive the 1980s recession. In 1986, Case I-H took it over completely.

THREE

DEERE & COMPANY

For John Deere, the modern era really began in 1960, when its beloved line of twin-cylinder tractors was finally dropped. Since the very early days of the Waterloo Boy, it had stuck to the principle that two horizontal cylinders were quite enough for any tractor. Unfortunately, the market didn't agree. The little twins might be simple, reliable, and economical, but farms were getting bigger. Buyers demanded more power, speed, and features. In theory, the twin could be enlarged to cope, but in practice the two cylinders would simply be too wide for row crop work.

There was only one answer, to design and build an all-new generation of tractors based around larger engines with more than two cylinders. So that's what they did, announcing a complete line of fours and sixes in one fell swoop. It wasn't just that the company came up with a full range, the new tractors were advanced as well. The six-cylinder 4010 and four-cylinder 3010 had power brakes and hydrostatic power steering. Smaller were the 1010 and 2010, built in Deere's Dubuque factory. Both

used four-cylinder engines, which on the 2010 had the option of gasoline, LPG, or diesel. And there was massive choice within the range. The smallest model alone came in ten different variations: seven row-crop tractors, an orchard, and two crawlers. If John Deere could have been accused of falling behind with its twin-cylinder policy, it now seemed that the opposite was true.

The larger two of the New Generation were soon updated into the 20 series, with more power and a Power Shift transmission (eight forward speeds, four reverse, and no clutching). The smaller ones followed suit in 1965, with the new 1020 gaining a three-cylinder engine, while the 2020 kept its four with balancer shafts. The shafts in the latter were an unusual feature; maybe years of experience with horizontal twins made John Deere impatient with the high frequency vibes of a four which other makers semed to accept as inherent. Meanwhile, the range was expanded both up and down as the 1960s progressed. American grain producers wanted more power,

A John Deere 6300 four-wheel-drive tractor. It is powered by the four-cylinder turbocharged 3.9-liter diesel engine rated at 90 PTO horsepower.

47

The John Deere 7520, produced between 1972 and 1974, was a big success, selling over 2,000 in a very specialized large four-wheel-drive articulated tractor market.

which the big 5020 provided (133 PTO hp), while exports to smaller European farms needed something more modest; three-cylinder 820 and 1520s were added, giving 31 and 46 hp, respectively.

But even the 5020 wasn't enough to keep up with the new breed of super-tractors with four-wheel-drive. Deere's immediate answer was to badge-engineer someone else's product, but in 1971 its own 7020 was unveiled. It followed the same theme as other super-tractors with an articulated chassis and the option of twin wheels all around; it was powered by a 145 hp intercooled diesel. A 175 hp 7520 followed in 1972. After three years, both were updated with yet more power—178 hp for the new 8430, 225 for the 8630. There was yet another (slight)

power hike in 1979, when both 4x4s became 40 series models. They acquired hydraulic differential locks and up to four remote hydraulic outlets.

Meanwhile, the New Generation was showing gray hairs, and Deere's response was the Generation II 30 series. Perhaps inevitably, they were more powerful than before, running through the 80 hp 4030, 100 hp 4230, turbocharged 4430 (125 hp), and intercooled 4630 with 150 hp. Hydrostatic front-wheel-drive was an option on all four, and there was a new trans-mission—16-speed Quad-Range was the name—though the old Power Shift was still available as an option, with clutches hydraulically controlled. But more obvious than any of this was the new styling—neater than before—and the Sound-Gard cab. This

John Deere's own 531-ci six-cylinder turbocharged and intercooled diesel engine, rated at 175 PTO horsepower at 2,100rpm, powers the 7520.

glassy, air conditioned command module was claimed to set new standards for in-cab refinement. One dealer later recalled how at the original launch, a film was shown with the presenter commentating from inside the cab; there was a gasp of astonishment when he climbed out, and they realized the engine had been running the whole time! It was hardly surprising that three out of four buyers opted for the new cab.

Small tractors weren't being neglected though, and the entry-level four- and three-cylinder Deeres (the latter now built at the Mannheim, Germany, factory) were updated into a 30 series with the lower-powered 830 (35 hp) and 1530 (45 hp) being added in 1973, as well as a range-topping 70 hp 2630.

Unlike the other small John Deeres, this one was built at the Dubuque plant. On all these smaller models, two-post Roll-Gard was an option, as it wasn't yet compulsory on all tractors. You could pay extra for a Quik-coupler hitch as well, plus the choice of 540/1,000rpm rear-mounted PTO or a mid-mounted 1,000rpm PTO.

The next upgrade came in 1975, when they were renamed (logically enough) the 40 series, with more power for the Mannheim three-cylinders; all the fours now came from the U.S. And like its rivals, John Deere looked to Japan for a competitive mini-tractor, signing a deal with Yanmar to produce a range of sub-40 hp machines. Unusually, these used Deere's own three-cylinder diesel rather than a Japanese one.

A John Deere 4040S tractor and New Holland 378 baler are hard at work in a hay field. The 4040S was built in the Bruchsal factory near Mannheim, West Germany, between 1981 and 1984. It uses the 359-ci six-cylinder John Deere turbocharged diesel engine.

In the difficult 1980s, as countless tractor dealers gave up the unequal struggle and many manufacturers found themselves merged, taken over, or closed down, John Deere seemed to survive by constant updating and the introduction of new models. The company's worldwide production base must have been a great help in those uncertain times, giving ready access to many different markets rather than being over-dependent on any one of them. Take the new 50 series, announced early in the decade. All five gave ten more PTO hp than the 40 series they replaced, and there was a new option of mechanical front-wheel-drive which allowed a tighter turning circle than the hydrostatic type. Most of the smaller models now hailed from Mannheim, and the new small 50 series ranged from the 45 hp 2150 to the 85 hp 2950. Sound-Gard cabs were optional, and all had transmissions capable of on-the-go shifting. Meanwhile, the successful Yanmar range was extended up to 62 hp, and there was a new small 900HC using Yanmar's own three-cylinder diesel. Aimed at nursery growers, it was the most economical tractor ever tested at Nebraska.

Then there was the 55 series, the smaller Mannheim models coming in 1987, and the Waterloo-built ones a couple of years later. Most had more power than before, in particular the 175 hp 4755, and the 4955, which was the first row crop tractor with 200 hp available at the PTO. Every model in the larger range had a turbo, and there were many engine changes. Power steps progressed through 105 hp to 120, 140, 155, and that range topping 200 hp, which produced its extra power thanks to an intercooler. Other new points were automatic engagement of the front-wheel-drive, the IntelliTrak monitoring system (Deere's version of electronic control), and electro-hydraulic hitch on the three largest tractors. Those three became the 60 series in 1992, but the differences were small. Engine power was unchanged, and the most significant feature seemed to be a slight redesign of the cab for better visibility and access. And there was a five year/5,000 hour warranty. Still, the company had other things on its mind in 1992.

The super-tractors were replaced by an all-new line of 60 series in 1988. Their engines were new, the wheelbase was longer, and even the Sound-Gard was redesigned (a new side access door allowed a wraparound one-piece windscreen with better visibility). The buyer was presented with three transmission options: 12-speed Synchro, Power Shift, or the 24-speed Powr-Sync with built-in Hi-Lo ranges. Enginewise, John Deere's own 304 hp V-8 was dropped in favor of a 14.0-liter 322 hp Cummins on the largest 8960, while smaller models made do with 7.6-liter (200 PTO hp) or 10.1-liter (256) diesels. And for the first time, triple wheels were an option.

This John Deere 4650 carries two front-mounted sprayer tanks and a rear planter. It is powered by a John Deere 466-ci six-cylinder turbocharged and intercooled diesel engine rated at 165.7 PTO horsepower.

This 1984 John Deere 8850 is Ruth Schaefer's own work tractor on the family farm at Grabill, Indiana. The immaculate 8850 has never suffered any problems or breakdowns in its 5,300 hours of work.

At the other end of the scale, something interesting was going on in Augusta, Georgia. During the calamatous 1980s, it seemed to become accepted wisdom that it was no longer possible to economically build small and mid-range tractors in the U.S. Yet in 1992 John Deere unveiled a complete new range of 40-60 hp machines, all made at a brand new factory in the South. All of these new 5000 series used three-cylinder diesels, one of which was turbocharged. All had hydrostatic power steering, nine-speed transmission, and optional four-wheel-drive.

Just after the 5000s appeared, there was, according to author Don MacMillan, "the most revolutionary development in John Deere tractor models since the New Generation multi-cylinder models replaced the two-cylinder line in 1960." It was the all-new 6000 and 7000 ranges, and for once, the term "all-new" fitted (though apparently nine components were carried over from the 60 series).

Certainly all of the engines were new. The four-cylinder 6000s (made in Mannheim) comprised the 75 hp 6100, 84 hp 6200, 90 hp 6300, and 100 hp 6400, the latter three all with turbos. But U.S. interest naturally settled on the six-cylinder 7000s, all of which were built at Waterloo. At launch, they came in three guises, the 6.8-liter 7600 (110 hp), 7.6-liter 7,700 (125 hp, and7.6-liter 7800 (140 hp). It wasn't just the engines that were new either; the transmission, hydraulics, cab,

A 1996 John Deere 6900 pulls a Claas Quadrant 1150 baler and sledge on the "Somerset levels" in Great Britain. The latest top-of-the-6000-range John Deere is powered by the six-cylinder 6.8-liter turbocharged diesel engine producing 130 PTO horsepower at 2,100rpm.

PTO, and electro-hydraulic hitch were all fresh off the drawing board as well. Take the cab. John Deere was keen to make a similar impact to the original Sound-Gard, and its new ComfortGard cab was claimed, at 72 dB, to be the quietest in the world. There was 40 percent more space than the Sound-Gard and 29 percent more glass area; the seat was air cushioned and the instrument panel tilted with the steering wheel, so drivers of whatever shape or size always got the same view.

In the mid-1990s, this joint Mannheim/Waterloo project formed the backbone of John Deere's range, but there were plenty of other models. The lower end of the market was at least partly covered by the 1750 and 1850, both of them powered by a 2.9-liter three-cylinder diesel. Power was the only difference between them, the 1850 developing an extra 6 hp from its higher-rated speed of 2,400rpm. It was a measure of how

A cross-section of the John Deere 7800 shows the four-wheel-drive and 19-speed powershift transmission. The six-cylinder turbocharged 7.636-liter John Deere diesel engine is rated at 170 horsepower. A dual-stage braking system with wet disc brakes stops this large tractor.

The 1996 John Deere 6600 four-wheel-drive tractor is powered by a six-cylinder turbocharged diesel engine rated at 113 PTO horsepower. This photo shows the sharp 52-degree steering angle and 12-degree castor angle. Combined, they accomplish tight turns.

The John Deere 3000 series is built by Renault in France but with three- and four-cylinder John Deere diesel engines. This 1996 3300X uses the four-cylinder 4.5-liter 75-horsepower diesel engine.

far the tractor market had come that even these relatively simple machines had clutchless shifting under load and a shuttle forward-reverse control. The latter device (a quick and simple change from forward to reverse and vice versa) has swept the tractor market for the simple reason that many tractors spend a lot of their time shuffling around in confined yards, despite all those brochure pictures of heroic plowing feats in massive fields under a big blue sky.

Meanwhile, the 6000 series had been extended upwards into the six-cylinder 6600/800/900. All these sixes were the company's own, and all were turbocharged; they included a 5.9-liter of 81 hp and a 6.8-liter giving 120 or 130 hp. The transmission was something called PowrQuad. This translated as four ranges (changeable under full load without clutching) and 20 speeds in all but the 6600; there was also a 24-speed option if you needed to sprint up to 25

The 1996 John Deere 6900 is fitted with the high-torque six-cylinder 6.8-liter 130 PTO horsepower John Deere diesel engine.

The 1996 John Deere 7600 four-wheel-drive tractor has the latest six-cylinder John Deere 6.8-liter turbocharged diesel engine producing 130 PTO horsepower.

mph. They all used the Perma-Clutch II, an oil-cooled multi-plate affair for which the makers claimed better temperature control than a conventional dry clutch.

So by the mid-1990s, John Deere seemed to have not only survived, but had every market segment covered. While the 6000 series was extended upwards, the 7000 came downwards to meet it, in 1993 there was yet another overseas agreement to increase the "long green line." Czech manufacturer Zetor would sell some of its low-price models as John Deeres in Asia, Australia, and Central and South America. If internationalism has been the John Deere strategy, it's certainly worked.

FOUR

FORD AND NEW HOLLAND

The Ford New Holland company is another recent corporate creation. Ford had been in the tractor business a long time, almost since the beginning, and bought up New Holland in 1986. It added Versatile to the group the following year, only to sell the whole lot to Fiat in 1991. But there seems to be no sign of any of these old names disappearing. The high-powered Genesis series, for example, was sold with a Ford badge; smaller tractors are called New Hollands; while the super-tractors are Versatiles. Fiat, meanwhile, has its own range.

Ford and New Holland

Ford as a company was no stranger to tractor design. Henry's Model T for the fields—the 1917 Fordson—introduced a new breed of lightweight, relatively cheap tractors that many small farmers could afford. Later highlights were the 9N, with Harry Ferguson's hydraulics, and the 8N, which used them without Mr Ferguson's permission. There followed a line of conventional, successful tractors. The post-war Fordson Major, for example, built at Dagenham, became Ford's most widely exported machine. Ford tended to concentrate on the smaller tractors, with models like the 3000, which offered 39 hp from Ford's own 2.9-liter three-cylinder diesel. Bigger models did come though, such as the 9000, launched in 1968, with a turbocharged six-cylinder engine of 6.5 liters.

Today, the range is about as wide as it could be, starting with the New Holland-badged 30 series. Baby of the range is the 3430, with 40 hp from a 3.2-liter non-turbo diesel (though there's also a turbo 4630 with 55 hp). Like many tractors of this size, it has three cylinders, which allows a shorter wheelbase and thus more maneuverability; there is a 62 hp four-cylinder 5030, but it's 6 inches longer. The transmission options are interesting, if only because it's only with these so-called utility tractors that you can still find a basic two-range setup with eight forward and two reverse speeds. The first upgrade (not actually available on the 3430) is an 8x8 shuttle, with

The Ford New Holland 7635 uses the 8000 series 3.9-liter turbocharged four-cylinder Fiat Iveco 95-horsepower engine. This Italian-built Ford New Holland wears colors that were first offered in February of 1996.

The Ford 8600 was manufactured between 1973 and 1977. Its 401-ci six-cylinder diesel engine was rated at 110 PTO horsepower at 2,300rpm.

instant selection of forward and reverse regardless of which gear you're in. Apart from the obvious benefit of extra reverse ratios, the shuttle gives an instant change of direction for, well, shuttling. Finally, there's the 16x8 version, which the maker calls DualPower. In effect, this doubles the number of forward ratios by giving a reduction of 20 percent or so on each one.

The 30 series looks like a traditional small tractor which could have been built any time in the last twenty years, but the one-step-up 35 is clearly much younger. Known as the L series in some markets, its low-nose front end and big glassy cab owe more to the 1990s than the 1970s. It also, interestingly enough, reflects the new Fiat ownership. It is powered by Iveco diesels; Iveco is a Fiat/Ford joint project of long standing, producing both engines and commercial vehicles. There's just one three-cylinder version (though unlike the 30 series threes, this one shares the same wheelbase as its more powerful brothers) with 60 hp at 2,500rpm. The four-cylinder range starts with the 4835 (3.6-liter, 65 hp) and ends at the 7635 (3.9-liter turbo with 95 hp).

As you'd expect, the transmissions on offer are more elaborate than those in the 30 series, starting with a 12x4 (four-speed synchromesh gearbox with three ranges) which allows a top speed of over 20 mph for road work. More modern tractors are now using extra-high ratios for more road speed. It's not just to satisfy speed-crazed drivers; there can be long

The Ford 8700 two-wheel-drive tractor was a redesign and update of the 8600 series. The 8700 series was introduced in 1977 to celebrate the sixtieth anniversary of Ford tractors.

road journeys between the far-flung parts of larger farms, while faster traffic on more congested roads (especially in Europe) makes more speed desirable. That's the basic transmission, though there is a shuttle option, powershift, and a creeper range. Steering is hydrostatic on all the 35 series, and four-wheel-drive is optional across the range. Options multiply for the PTO as well, with a choice of mechanical, dry plate, or hydraulic multi-plate clutches and 6- or 21-spline output shafts. Also, an increasingly common feature on current tractors, the 540rpm PTO speed has an economy setting for lighter work at reduced engine speed. Finally, the PTO can be synchronized to the tractor's ground speed.

With the 40 series, we move into the upper-medium part of the range, still wearing the New Holland badge. Reaching into the 100 hp plus sector, the 40 series marks the beginning of serious power, where four-wheel-drive is mandatory at the upper end of the range, and electronics put in an

The 1977 Ford 8700 diesel engine was an updated version of the 401-ci six-cylinder Ford engine introduced in 1968 in the 8000 series tractor.

The Ford FW-30 articulated four-wheel-drive tractor was built by Steiger Tractor, Inc., of Fargo, North Dakota, and marketed by Ford.

appearance. The engine choice shifts from threes and fours to fours and sixes, with the most powerful of each being turbocharged. The mid-range 7740, for example, uses a 5.0-liter turbo four with 95 hp, while the range-topping 8340 has 125 hp from its 7.5-liter six. There's also a 100 hp non-turbo six (smaller, at 6.6 liters). These big ranges, with multiple small power steps, are something common to most tractor makers, reflecting the multiplicity of roles demanded of the modern tractor. It's the same with transmissions. This particular tractor can be had with 12x12 syncromesh ratio, which of course is doubled to 24x24 if you opt for powershift. Then there's the electronically controlled Electroshift (16x16), which rises to 24x24 with an optional creeper set of ratios. Tractor options are routinely so complex that it's probably true that few tractors come off the line with identical specifications.

Moving up a class again, we come to the 60 series, and it's back to the modern low-nose look for this very recently launched machine. At this sort of power (100-160 hp), six-cylinders are the norm, in

A Ford 7840 Powerstar SL with the 12x12 synchroshift transmission. This 1990s Series 40 Ford New Holland tractor was built by the new N.H. Geotech company.

this case all of the same 7.6-liter capacity. Designed to meet the 1997 EPA emissions regulations, the Gemini engine, as the maker calls it, has a "snail shell" inlet port to encourage good swirl and mixing within the cylinder, while the piston has a combustion bowl. New Holland claims a more constant power output than other tractors, but then that's what they all claim. The ideal for a tractor is to have as wide a spread of power as possible, to keep pulling strongly from very low speeds. You're unlikely to find a tractor maker who doesn't claim that its particular product is great at doing just that.

The 8160 kicks the 8000 range off, with the 100 hp (measured by the EEC method) non-turbo

engine, and progresses through the 8260 (115 hp), 8360 (135), and 8560 (160); the latter two are both turbocharged. The 8560's standard transmission (optional on the others) is an 18x6 with six gearbox speeds in three ranges. The maker recommends the lowest range (1.4 to 3.5 mph) be used for row crop cultivation, the mid-range (3.2 to 8.0 mph) for harvesting and tillage, and the high range (9.1 to 22.7 mph) for light loads and road work. Power shift (push-button clutchless shifting) tends to be standard on this class of tractor, as it is on this one. It's also possible to change between ranges on the move. At low speeds, the tractor will automatically stop for a second to make the change, and the clutch is then fed in automatically for a smooth restart. With electronics, you can have features like a programable reverse. To complete the up-to-the-minute image, an electronic digital dashboard is optional on the two turbocharged 60 series.

The top of the Ford New Holland range is the 70 series, which unlike the others is actually badged as a Ford. Here again, power comes from a family of 7.5-liter six-cylinder diesels, but with more of it than in the 60 series. There are 170/190 hp turbo versions, or 210/240 hp with intercooling. The 18 forward and 9 reverse speed transmission runs up to 25 mph and has an automatic setting. Once you've pressed the appropriate button (plenty to choose from in the 70 series cab), and in 10th gear, the transmission will automatically shift up at 2,100rpm and down again at 1,600. Or by depressing the inching pedal (there is no clutch pedal), the transmission will select the gear that best suits your speed and load. Times have changed since the 9N.

Versatile

Versatile played much the same role as Steiger, an early specialist manufacturer of four-wheel-drive super-tractors. The D118, launched in 1967, was one of the smaller ones, with 140 hp claimed for its 5.7-liter Cummins V-6. The 800 of 1975 was more typical of what super-tractors had become after a decade of the horsepower race. It used a massive 13.9-liter Cummins straight six for which Versatile claimed 235 hp (at the flywheel, not the PTO). It had 12 forward speeds, with a range of 2.6-14.3 mph.

But just like Steiger, Versatile couldn't remain independent forever, and in 1987 (the year after Steiger sold out, strangely enough), it was taken over by Ford New Holland, which needed access to some super-tractor technology to complete its range. As a result, Versatile simply became the name for the Ford combine's 4x4 range, and as the years went by, it got relegated to a minor script on the hood, overshadowed

The New Holland 7840 tractor carries the New Holland tree motif on the front of the hood and the Ford name in small letters on the side.

by FORD in big letters. To confuse things further, it was still sold as a New Holland product.

By 1995, the Versatile range, whatever the dealers liked to call it, consisted of the 80 series, a line of four super-tractors with twin wheels and big power outputs. Like Steiger, the Versatiles had turned to Cummins for its big diesels, and the range now went

In 1995, the bold-letter Ford name appeared for the last time on the side of a 7840 series tractor. The 401-ci six-cylinder diesel engine was rated at 100 horsepower.

was 1,330 lb ft of torque at 1,400rpm. The twin fuel tanks held 245 U.S. gallons; the axles alone needed 12.7 U.S. gallons of lubricant, and there was almost 16 U.S. gallons of coolant. And the maximum operating weight of the tractor was 40,000 lb. Standard transmission was a 12 forward, 4 reverse unit using three ranges (Quadra-sync was the name), and a 12x2 powershift was optional on the mid-range 9000s. But really, these transmissions were simpler than the multi-speed, creeper and shuttle units used on smaller tractors. Super-tractors had no need for ultra-low speed crawler gears, and their size made them a little unsuited to back-and-forth shuffling in the yard. If double wheels weren't enough, triples were an option. Versatile might no longer be independent, but its name lived on (in a small way) on the hood of an up-to-date super-tractor.

Fiat

Well before it bought Ford New Holland, Fiat had its own comprehensive range of tractors. Why then, spend all that money? There is at least one possible explanation. The Italian company had a successful working relationship with Allis-Chalmers, having sold its 50 hp machine in the U.S. with A-C badges from 1976 to 1983. There were plans to replace it with newer Fiat 50 and 60 hp tractors, but this fell through when A-C was sold to Deutz. So Fiat was left without access to the massive U.S. tractor market, depressed though it was. Owning Ford New Holland would give access to many U.S. tractor dealers. Another benefit was immediate access to large modern tractors to extend the Fiat range. If Fiat's G series looks exactly like a rebadged, repainted Ford 70 series, that's because it is.

Meanwhile, Fiat's massive range of conventional, uncomplicated tractors has continued. In 1993, the little 66S series three-cylinder tractors started off with a real baby of 1,551cc and 35 hp. Despite having the same 66 tag as the rest of this series, it was smaller than all of them, with a shorter wheelbase

as follows: 9280, 250 hp 10.0-liter turbo; 9480, 300 hp 14.0-liter turbo/intercooled; 9680 350 hp 14.0-liter turbo/intercooled; 9880, 400 hp, 14.0-liter turbo/intercooled.

Lists of figures can get boring, but a few more from the 9880's spec sheet show just how big these tractors had become. As well as that 400 hp, there

A 1996 Ford New Holland 7740 pulls a New Holland 640 round baler. The 304-ci 5-liter engine is rated in Europe at 95 horsepower.

and narrower track. But you still had a 16x16 transmission, 540/1,000rpm PTOs, and power steering. The top of this range was the 60-66S, with a (as you'd expect) 60 hp 2.9-liter engine and a 20x12 transmission on the options list. It also had nearly three times the lift capacity of its baby brother. All five 66 series Fiats were available with four-wheel-drive and a cab optional on all except the 35.

Next up came a range of three four-cylinder 66s, from a 3.6-liter (65 or 70 hp) to an 80 hp 3.9-liter. All these engines, incidentally, are Fiat's own; one advantage of being a massive corporation is never having to buy engines from outside. Dimensionally bigger than the threes, the four-cylinder 66s had very similar specifications, apart from a higher lift capacity. You'd also need to be especially eagle-eyed to spot that the 70 and 80 hp ones used slightly larger wheels as well.

The 93 series moves up half a class, rather than a whole one. It is only slightly bigger than the 66, and uses the same engine range as most of the 66s as well, the three-cylinder 2.9-liter and 3.6/3.9-liter fours. The only real difference enginewise is the availability of a turbocharged version of the 3.9, which produces 85 hp at 2,500rpm. The PTO is sychronized to ground speed, though 540, 750, and 1,000rpm options are available. The 94 series has slightly different styling than the 93, but is really a slightly updated version of the same thing. Same size, same 60-85 hp diesels, but with various cab options (including air conditioning) and an electro-hydraulic differential lock.

Near the top of Fiat's home-grown tractors is the 90 series, starting with the Central Range of 100-110 hp tractors. They all used non-turbo six-cylinder

67

This 1980 Versatile 555 uses the 555-ci Cummins V-8 diesel engine producing 210 horsepower. Fuel tank capacity is 185 gallons.

diesels, of 5.4 or 5.8-liter, with a standard 15x3 transmission (a 20x4 was optional). Four-wheel-drive was standard, but you had to pay extra for the Super-Comfort cab. All 90 series tractors were turbocharged. But in styling terms at least, the 90 series looked rather dated by 1990s standards, with its severe, rectangular hood and square-rigged cab.

More contemporary looking was the F series, which was lower-powered than the 90 (the top one used the High Range 90's lowest-powered engine), but

came with an unheard-of range of transmission options. The basic setup was a fairly unremarkable 16x16, but there were creeper options, Eco-Speed, and a choice of 19 or 25 mph top speed. So if you needed something with 32 reverse speeds and 64 forwards, your tractor awaited. So Fiat had a big range of tractors (we haven't even mentioned the Lift-O-Matic, vineyard, orchard, and low profile versions, or the crawlers). It'll be interesting to see how it integrates with the similarly large selection offered by Ford New Holland.

A Ford New Holland 5635. The Fiat L and New Holland 5635 series tractors are built in Italy by Fiatagri. This model uses the Fiat Iveco naturally aspirated diesel 75-horsepower four-cylinder engine of 3.9 liters.

The Versatile 895 is powered by a six-cylinder turbocharged Cummins 855-ci diesel engine rated at 310 horsepower.

This 1994 Fiatagri F140 wears the New Holland badge on the radiator surround. Farmer Alan Britten is hard at work with the powerful top-of-the-line tractor on his farm in Somerset, Great Britain.

This Fiatagri 88-94 tractor has the turbocharged four-cylinder 3.9-liter diesel engine rated at 85 PTO horsepower at 2,500rpm.

FIVE

OTHER TRACTOR COMPANIES

JCB

For years in England, JCB meant only one thing: bright yellow diggers with a scoop at each end, usually seen on building sites and construction projects. So successful were they that JC Bamford Excavators, Ltd., monopolized the market for a while. The generic term for a digger, any digger, was "JCB." But inevitably, rivals came up with their own diggers, and JCB needed a new idea to keep ahead.

It came in 1991, as the Fastrac, a new type of high-speed tractor that could hit an unheard of 45 mph on the road. Most tractors are limited to half that speed or less, so where long road hauling jobs came in, the Fastrac promised to give substantial time (and therefore money) savings over a conventional tractor.

It's an odd looking thing, part truck, part tractor, though the specification reads mcuh the same as any other tractor. Power for the current Fastrac 155 comes from Perkins' 1006-6T4, which gives 150 hp at 2,400rpm and 444 lb ft at 1,400rpm. There's a six-speed gearbox with three ranges and a two-speed splitter, which adds up to 36 forward and 12 reverse ratios. The PTO gives 540/1,000rpm and there are disc brakes all around.

But look more closely and you'll see the differences. The air brakes are actually to truck specification, and despite having 36 ratios, the Fastrac has no ultra-low crawler range. The suspension is remarkably soft by tractor standards and is self-leveling at the rear. The front uses conventional coil springs, but at the rear there are gas-filled accumulators and hydraulic cylinders. The result, says JCB, is better traction, a constant ride height, and a smoother ride.

The Fastrac concept has evidently done well for JCB, as there's now a big range of them. The smallest models are the short wheelbase 1115 and 1135; they are powered by a naturally aspirated or turbocharged Perkins six-cylinder diesel (115 or 135 hp), though these can manage a mere 31 mph on the road. The mid-range 135/155 are Perkins-powered too, and have that 45 mph capability. More horse-

A Renault 80.14 Herdsman pulls a spreader. The four-cylinder, air-cooled Deutz diesel engine of 4,086cc produces 76 horsepower at 2,350rpm.

The JCB Fastrac 155 high-speed tractor has a street-legal 45 mph road speed. It is powered by a high-torque Perkins 6-liter, six-cylinder diesel engine rated at 150 horsepower.

power is on offer from the 185, which uses a 5.9-liter Cummins (turbocharged and intercooled) straight six of 170 hp/532 lb ft.

But a more significant new model appeared in 1996, the Quadtronic. Based on the smaller 1115 and 1135, it added four-wheel steering. Some high-performance cars have used this as a handling aid, but JCB claimed that it would make the Fastrac far more

maneuverable than any other tractor. As well as simply turning the wheel, the driver has five steering options: conventional two-wheel steer (the front wheels only); true tracking (both axles steer together following the

A JCB Fastrac 135 high-speed road tractor can pull a six-bottom plow. The six-cylinder Perkins engine is rated at 135 horsepower at 2,400rpm.

same line); proportional tracking (rear axle turns 1 degree for every 2 degrees of front axle turn); delay mode (front axle turns up to 20 degrees before the rear starts to turn); and most bizarre of all, crab steer (both axles steer in the same direction) which, as the name suggests, allows the tractor to move diagonally like a crab. If nothing else, it shows that there are still some new ideas in tractor development.

Matbro

In the early days, one tractor was expected to do everything. How times have changed. Few farms now rely on just one machine, and many buy more specialized machines suited to particular tasks.

Take the Matbro, which has but one natural habit: shunting in the yard. Neither of the axles steer; instead, the whole thing is articulated to give a tight turning circle in confined spaces. It's really a super-forklift, able to lift up to 2.5 tons at a time in the front loader. Made in a little factory in the English Cotswolds, it comes with Perkins 4.0-liter diesels of 75, 96, or 106 hp; has four-wheel-drive; and a torque convertor transmission. In the top-of-the-range TR250, this includes a Clark powershift system with four forward speeds and three reverse, plus electronic selection. You wouldn't use a Matbro for plowing, but then that's not what it's for.

Renault

Renault is one of the lower-profile tractor producers, without the big worldwide presence of a John Deere or Massey-Ferguson. And unlike these instantly recognizable names, it wasn't even set up to make tractors. Louis Renault was a motoring pioneer, and the company's first tractor was really a converted tank!

77

The Matbro TR250 tractor loader is powered by a four-cylinder 106-horsepower Perkins engine. Matbro, Ltd., of Tetbury, Gloucestershire, Great Britain, sells a wide variety of loader tractors.

The Matbro TR200 loader tractor uses the high-torque agricultural 1000 series Perkins diesel engine. With excellent visibility and maneuverability, these loader tractors have sold in large numbers in Europe.

The HI crawler had a 20 hp gasoline engine and a three forward/one reverse gear transmission. It did without the tank's armor-plating but retained its caterpillar tracks. A wheeled version—the HO—followed a few years later. It wasn't until 1927 that something closer to a pure agricultural tractor appeared. The PE was again powered by a 20 hp gas engine, but advances included a spring-damped towing hitch. Six years later, the VY and YL tractors appeared. These were very advanced for their time, with diesel power, rubber tires, and a dry disc clutch. Machines like this enabled Renault to capture one third of the small French tractor market between the wars.

In the late 1940s, with Renault now state-owned, the 3040 series was the main range; it claimed to be the first production tractor with a full electrical system. It also had a second PTO speed, hydraulic lift with position control, and variable wheel track. As in the rest of Europe, there was a huge pent-up demand for farm mechanization after the war, and Renault soon felt constrained by its Billancourt factory. So the newer Le Mans factory was revamped and has been the home of Renault tractors ever since.

As the postwar years progressed, Renault's offerings in the tractor market advanced along with everyone elses, though the D series of 1956 was unusual in offering air-cooled as well as water-cooled diesel power. There was a differential lock, syncromesh gearbox, and a 540rpm PTO, but the three-point hitch had to wait until the Super D series of 1965. Other 1960s innovations were torque converters, the tracto-control, and four-wheel-drive. Like other manufacturers, Renault paid more attention to in-cab comfort in the late 1960s, especially with anti-vibration measures and the heating system.

Nineteen seventy-four saw the launch of a complete range of new machines, from 30 to 115 hp.

A Renault 80.14 Herdsman pulls a spreader. The four-cylinder, air-cooled Deutz diesel engine of 4,086cc produces 76 horse-power at 2,350rpm.

The Renault 155.54 Turbo uses a six-cylinder, water-cooled turbocharged diesel engine rated at 145 horsepower. This model is fitted with the Tractronic transmission which gives 24 forward and 8 reverse speeds.

There were two- and four-wheel-drive versions, and the innovation of the forward and reverse shuttle transmission to give easy changes of direction. Now a standard feature on many modern tractors, the ideal is to provide push-button selection of forward and reverse without having to grapple with the main gear lever.

But much of Renault's development work in the 1980s seemed concerned with bettering the driver's environment—the cab. The TX cab was launched in 1981 and offered a passenger seat, roof hatch, and work lights, as well as good visibility.

There was an economy (TS) version of the same thing, but it shared at least one of the TX's innovations. Both cabs could be raised clear of the transmission in less than an hour, using a set of jacks, but the engine and hydraulics would still run. This is normally a major operation involving an overhead crane and removal of the wheels. Going in the other direction, the RS cab of 1984 was simply a low-profile version of the same, mirroring Massey-Ferguson's practice of offering low-profile and "hi-line" cabs.

A Renault 160.94 TZ Multi-Shift with a four-meter power harrow drill combination unit. Renault tractors are built at the Renault Agriculture factory at Le Mans in the La Sarthe region of France.

Continuing with the cab theme, the TZ of 1987 isolated the cab and driver from the rest of the tractor, not by rubber blocks, but a system of springs and shock absorbers. It was a crossover from Renault's experience in the truck field, where isolated cabs were just as desirable. But if anyone thought that tractor drivers were getting soft, they'd seen nothing yet. Nineteen ninety-one saw the Nectra. Based on the TZ cab, there were also electronic aids, gold paintwork, and leather trim.

In the mid-1990s, much of Renault's business comes from the 54 series High Range. In the U.K., there were five engine options, all of them water-cooled MWM diesels. The sole four-cylinder option was a 4.2-liter turbo of 93 hp, while the 6.2-liter six went up from 100 hp to 110, 123, and 145. Surprisingly, only the most powerful of these was turbocharged. TX and TZ cabs were offered on all the six-cylinder tractors and there was, of course, all the usual features of a modern machine. "Tractorradar," for example, was Renault's version of the electronic monitoring of work operations that every tractor maker was adopting in some shape or

This Renault 180.94 TZ Turbo is teamed with a Claas Quadrant 1200 square baler. The Multi-Shift transmission has 9 speeds in three ranges, giving 27 forward and 27 reverse speeds.

form. In this guise, it used a radar sensor to measure the true ground speed and compared this to the theoretical speed to calculate wheelspin. In contact with the electronic lower link, this makes continuous height adjustments of the draft level to keep wheelspin to a pre-determined level. It also keeps an eye on distance covered and area worked.

But if the 54 series' conventional 16 forward and 16 reverse gear transmission wasn't enough, the 160/180 tractors, launched in 1993, offered another development. It was the Multishift transmission with its 27 speeds and fully clutchless changes. There are three ranges (Creep, Field, and Travel, denoted respectively by a snail, tortoise, and hare), each with nine speeds ranging from a brisk 24 mph down to a genuinely snail-like 545 yph. Instead of the usual gear levers, the driver is presented with two T-bar levers which look as if they've been plucked straight out of an automatic car. All the changes are electronically controlled, and the rear differential lock, PTO, and four-wheel-drive are all push-button operated.

Engine options are uprated versions of the MWM 6.2, with 150 or 170 hp.

The Multishift tractor looks relatively conventional, but the lower-powered Ceres, announced at the same time, is very different. In this lower-powered machine (55-95 hp), the direct-injection diesels are three or four cylinders of 2.9-4.5 liters, and the transmission starts with a basic 10 forward and 10 reverse unit. But in typical Renault fashion, there's the option of the X cab, with its digital dashboard and quieter ambience.

With all this talk of hi-tech cabs and transmissions, we shouldn't forget the small Renault tractors, the fruit and vineyard versions which have a particular following in their native country. Built small and narrow, these still use the Deutz air-cooled diesel, starting with a three-cylinder 52 hp unit of 2.8 liters. You won't find complex electronic controls here, but these little tractors are simple and maneuverable. The Herdsman tractors are really general purpose versions of the Renaut, but aimed at livestock farms.

Or there's the Groundsman, which has much the same power, but with tires more suited to parks and gardens.

SAME

Ferguson had Harry, Fordson had Henry, and SAME's founder, inspiration, and leading light was Francesco Cassani. The son of a mechanic, there was little doubt that the young Cassani would follow his father into engineering. His first project was a home-built car powered by a left-over aero engine! But a far more serious project was to follow, which was to make Francesco famous not just in his home province of Bergamo, but throughout Italy.

With his younger brother Eugenio, Francesco began experimenting with their own version of the diesel engine. Diesel had already established itself in the big engine market, but no one had yet applied it to tractors. So in 1924, the Cassani became the world's first diesel tractor. It was said to cut running costs by 60 percent, but the course of innovation rarely runs smoothly. The Cassani took several years to get even close to production. When it did, the company contracted to build it promptly collapsed. Francesco decided to forget about tractors for a while, but returned to the fold in 1945 with SAME (Societa Anonima Motori Endotermici).

Innovations followed, notably a small 10 hp three-wheeler in 1948 which had a reversible seat so that the driver could check how rear-mounted implements were doing. Just as significant for modern machinery was the world's first four-wheel-drive tractor in 1952. As modern tractors gained weight and power, traction became more critical; four-wheel-drive was the only answer, and it's now almost universal. Unlike many rivals, SAME has managed to stay independent, taking over Lamborghini tractors in 1972 and the Swiss-based Hurlimann five years later.

Although SAME has followed rivals into the market for mini-tractors, powered either by Mitsubishi diesels or its own air-cooled three-cylinder, more

The body and cab on the 1995 SAME Silver 90 tractor are designed by the famous Italian designer Giugiaro, better known for his car and pasta creations.

relevant to our interest is the Explorer II, SAME's bread-and-butter mid-range tractor. Its most recent update has been the 1000 series engine, which according to SAME is fitted to all of its tractors except the minis. Like rivals, it has made the most of a modular range, simply changing the bore and stroke sizes and the number of cylinders to give a wide range of engines with many parts in common. Not only is the result cheaper to make and stock parts for, but it gives a massive range, from the Dorado 60's three-cylinder, 3.0-liter (60 hp) to the Titan 160, whose engine is twice as big and almost twice as powerful. Unusual in a modern tractor, the 1000 series is air-cooled, with oil cooling for the cylinder block.

In the Explorer, it comes in both turbo and non-turbo form up to the 90 hp class. There's also the modern, round hood Dorado, which uses what the maker calls Agroshift, a five-speed gearbox with three ranges. Range changes are made without the clutch. The 80-100 hp Silver has the same modern

A 1995 SAME Silver 90 turbocharged Agroshift with forage harvester. The SAME 1000.4 A4 four-cylinder engine is rated at 90 horsepower at 2,500rpm.

styling and the same Agroshift with electronic control of the four-wheel-drive. Interestingly, there are two versions of the 100 hp Silver: four-cylinder 4.0-liter turbo or six-cylinder 6.0-liter aspirated. The SAME Antres occupies the 100 hp-plus class and comes in six-cylinder form only. A turbocharged version of that 6.0-liter engine gives 127 hp at 2,500rpm and 345 lb ft at 1,300rpm. It also has an astonishing 72-speed transmission. Not only is there a six-speed gearbox with four ranges (creeper, slow, medium, and high), but each ratio has a push button which gives an immediate 20 percent shift up or down; in other words, from nearly 25 mph right down to 0.1 mph.

SAME's Titan range doesn't have quite that many ratios (27 forward or reverse), but it is the most powerful on offer. The 1000 series six is intercooled to give 145, 159, or 189 hp. As in the latest generation of diesel cars, the injection is electronically controlled (trucks have been using this for some time) for more efficient running, and like all the SAMEs, it can run on biodiesel.

There are other SAME innovations. These include things like the Automatic Power Shift, a

The door decals on this 1990 SAME Antares 100 tell everyone that the air-cooled SAME engine is turbocharged and intercooled to produce 100 horsepower.

fully automatic gearbox for tractors. Or there's the Global Monitor, which uses a roof-mounted camera to give the driver a permanent view of what's going on behind. It's a long way from Francesco Cassani's first diesel, but he would probably approve.

Valmet

Of all the tractor makers featured here, Valmet is one of the youngest. Unlike most, it has no 19th century roots or long association with agriculture. Instead, Valtion Metallitehtaat (soon shortened to Valmet) was set up after World War II to build something more constructive out of the Finnish munitions industry. It was a real swords into plowshares operation, making use of a former rifle factory, which was versed in precision engineering and mass production. In fact, on the prototypes, the clutch and gearbox were connected by a cannon bore!

From those first prototypes of 1949, production slowly built up to 75 tractors in 1952, 850 the year after, and 2,000 in 1954. The tractor was the Valmet 15, a lightweight machine with a little sidevalve 1.5-liter engine that ran on kerosene and produced 15

85

This 1990 SAME Antares Turbo 100 has proven to be economical and reliable on Bruce Whittle's dairy farm at Bagley, Somerset, Great Britain.

hp at 2,000rpm. To keep up the peace dividend theme, it was built by a factory that had made aircraft engines during the war.

The Valmet 15 was a success in tractor-starved postwar Finland, but it soon became clear that more power was needed to keep up with the competition. A 20 hp version followed and in 1957 came the 33D, with Valmet's own three-cylinder diesel. Direct-injection was chosen for its better cold starting ability in Scandanavian winters; there were those who wanted air cooling as well, to prevent freeze-ups, but Finland has hot summers too, so the 33D was water-cooled.

A Brazilian satellite factory was up and running by the end of 1960, the same year in which the new 361D appeared. Like other tractor makers, Valmet was waking up to the importance of styling. The new tractor, with its modern, squared-off hood, had an uprated version of the three-cylinder diesel with 42 hp. Bigger Valmets followed, including a four-cylinder diesel, the 363D four-wheel-drive forest tractor, and the 80 hp Valmet 80. In 1967, the new 900 made an impact with its attention to ergonomics. The tractor featured an integral safety cab that was rubber-mounted; it had low (by 1960s standards) noise levels. The steering was hydrostatic and visibility was fine. It was soon followed by Valmet's first turbo, the 115 hp 1100. Opinions differ as to whether Valmet or Volvo built Europe's first turbocharged tractor.

That engine was also featured in the 1102, which replaced the 900/1100 in 1973. But a real departure was the six-wheeled 1502 bogie tractor. In it, the rear wheels were replaced with a bogie of four driven wheels; this system was designed to reduce ground pressure and increase speeds. With a 136 hp turbo six, it took Valmet into a new class of tractor.

The Valmet 8050 is the smallest-capacity tractor in the Mega 50 series. The Valmet Permatorque six-cylinder turbocharged 6.6-liter engine is rated at 110 horsepower.

There were more technical firsts to come, including the first turbocharged three-cylinder diesel, a low-pressure turbo to reduce smoke levels, and a Comprex supercharged four. The latter, being driven directly be the engine, eliminated turbo lag and offered excellent pulling power at low engine speeds.

It was about this time when an agreement was signed with Volvo to cooperate on the next new tractor in the 65-100 hp class. Both companies would share one model. Prototypes of the so-called Nordic tractor first ran in 1980, and went on sale only two years later. Styled by Volvo, it had the wedge-shaped hood which has since become standard for modern tractors. The range was big, from the two-wheel-drive non-turbo 504 to the 95 hp 805. The six-cylinder 905 soon followed, in 105 hp non-turbo form, as well as the smaller 305 and 405. All of these were sold either as Volvo BM Valmets or just plain Valmets, though in 1985 Valmet bought its partner out of the joint venture. From then on, the tractors were badged Valmet only.

Three years later Valmet caused a real stir in the tractor world by offering a choice of colors. Traditionally, each tractor maker has had its own color—green/black for Deutz, the Persian Orange of Allis—but Valmet was now offering five different colors. Still, it looks as if this is one Valmet innovation that has not swept the industry. Of more significance to most buyers was the Power Plus range of 1988, which brought more power for most of the range, including a new 455 with a 3.3-liter turbocharged three of 67 hp.

The current range keeps a presence among smaller tractors with the three-cylinder 365/465; all of them are available with four-wheel-drive. But like most its rivals, Valmet has had to cater to the big power tractor buyers as well. The Mega 50 range tractors all use a six-cylinder diesel, of 6.6 or 7.4 liters, and all have turbos. The mid-range 8450 has 140 hp at 2,200rpm and 428 lb ft at 1,450rpm. The transmission is a 36-speed forward and reverse with,

as you'd expect, shuttle change and creeper gears. In keeping with its ergonomic past, Valmet places great stress on the cab. It's called TwinTrac, which means two sets of controls so that the driver can swivel through 180 degrees to work looking forwards or backwards. There's even a soft-feel steering wheel which wouldn't look out of place in a luxury car! The 8450 has a digital Agrodata display to show things like PTO speed, oil temperature, and height of the lower links. And as on every other big tractor these days, electronics are used to ease the workload, an example being the slip limiter, which raises the implement if excess slippage is detected. If the 6.6-liter 8450 doesn't have enough power, the 8750, with 7.4 liters and 190 hp (plus 605 lb ft), is Valmet's answer.

In 1994, Valmet was taken over by the Finnish Sisu group, though the Valmet name stays on the hood. In these days of multi-takeovers, this retention of national independence is quite an achievement.

Zetor

Before the fall of the Berlin Wall, the products of Eastern Europe had a certain reputation, and it's stuck, despite the political revolution since then. They were basic and unsophisticated, as well as solid and of good value. Czechoslovakia (now divided into Slovakia and the Czech Republic) has done well out of this, selling cars from Skoda, motorcycles by Jawa-CZ, and Zetor tractors.

Tractors were being made in Czechoslovakia in the 1920s, but the twin-cylinder Zetor didn't appear until 1945. Three- and four-cylinder versions were launched in 1960, and made their U.K. debut six years later. In those days, Zetor still sourced some components from the West. Clutch and brake parts, for example, were British on some Zetors, while hydraulic lifts and rear axle components were sourced within Eastern Europe. Since then, Zetor has taken the unusual step of making almost every part of its tractors in-house.

The Valmet Mega 8800 uses the six-cylinder, turbocharged, 190-horsepower, 7.4-liter Valmet diesel engine. The tractor's transmission has 36 forward and reverse speeds.

The range was restyled in the late 1960s, and the famous Chrystal range was launched in 1969. And in updated form, some of these tractors are what Zetor still makes today. Take the Unified One range, which originated in the early 1960s. It has been recently updated and covers the low- to mid-range. It kicks off with the 3320 and 3340 (the "4" signifies four-wheel-drive), both powered by Zetor's own three-cylinder direct-injection diesel. The engine deserves a mention; being based on the modular principle, it includes a wide range of sizes (from the 2.7-liter three to a 3.9-liter turbocharged four) by juggling with just two different bore and stroke sizes.

As it's sold partly on price, the Unified One isn't as well-equipped as some tractors (the 3320/3340 have just a single-range five-speed transmission, and even the radio is extra!). But this is what you expect from a budget tractor like the Zetor, and in any case, it is possible to upgrade the basic spec with shuttle and creeper transmissions, while hydrostatic steering is standard across the range.

The Valmet 1502 six-wheel-drive tractor is designed for high-speed work and low ground pressure. Power comes from the Valmet 6.6-liter, 136-horsepower, six-cylinder diesel engine.

A 1985 Volvo BM Valmet 2105. These tractors were produced by the merger of the Volvo and Valmet companies. The Volvo TD 60 K turbocharged and intercooled 5.5-liter engine produces 163 horsepower.

A Zetor 7540 four-wheel-drive tractor pulls a Zetor AUR55 spreader. The 7520 two-wheel-drive and 7540 four-wheel-drive both use the Zetor type 7801 four-cylinder, 71-horsepower diesel engine.

A more recent addition is the Compact Tractor, with standard four-wheel-drive and—a real departure for Zetor—an engine bought in from outside (a 1.5-liter 33 hp Lombardini diesel). The Compact isn't really designed for farm work at all, but more for parks and tree nursuries. The Unified Three range is another relatively recent addition, this time a traditional mid-range tractor using Zetor's 4.1-liter diesel with or without turbo and intercooler. The transmission on the top-range 10540 comprises 18 forward speeds through a three-speed gearbox in two ranges with a three-stage torque multiplier. At the top of Zetor's range

come the six-cylinder tractors, all with four-wheel-drive and a 6.8-liter engine. The transmission is different again, this time with a four-speed box, two ranges, and two-stage torque multiplier.

Unlike much of Czech industry, Zetor has not been taken over by foreign investors since the fall of the Wall. It was privatized, but resisted a foreign takeover bid and is now owned by a Czech bank. With its independence intact, and a strong relationship with John Deere (about 25 percent of Zetor production is sold straight to the American firm), Zetor looks like it will produce its range of good-value tractors for some time yet.

The Zetor 7540 four-wheel-drive tractor uses the liquid-cooled, 4.156-liter, four-cylinder Zetor diesel engine.

INDEX